The Historic Significance of the Southern Revolution

The Historic Significance of the Southern Revolution:
A Lecture Delivered by Invitation in Petersburg, Va.,
March 14th and April 29th, 1864,
and in Richmond, Va., April 7th and April 21st, 1864

By

William A. Hall

Prepared for Publication
By
HISTORIC PULISHING
San Antonio, Texas

The Historic Significance of the Southern Revolution

THE HISTORIC SIGNIFICANCE OF THE SOUTHERN REVOLUTION. A LECTURE

Delivered by Invitation in Petersburg, Va, March 14th and April 29th, 1864. And in Richmond, Va., April 7th and April 21st, 1864.

BY

REV. WILLIAM A. HALL

OF NEW ORLEANS
BATTALION WASHINGTON ARTILLERY.

PETERSBURG:

LARGE PRINT EDITION

PRINTED BY A. F. CRUTCHFIELD & CO., BANK, STREET, 1864.

The Historic Significance of the Southern Revolution

CORRESPONDENCE

HEAD-QUARTERS BATTALION WASHINGTON ARTILLERY,
Near Petersburg, Va., May 2nd, 1864.

Rev. Wm. A. Hall, Chaplain B W. A.:

DEAR SIR:--In accordance with the expressed wish of many members of the Battalion, and of many gentlemen of Petersburg and Richmond who have heard your Lecture on the *"Historic Significance of the Southern Revolution,"* we desire to obtain a copy of it for publication. Believing that a wide-spread dissemination of your well matured views, on a subject of such import, will be conducive of much good to our great cause, and hoping our request will meet your approbation.

We are, sir, with sincere regard, Your Obedient Servants,

E. S. DREW, *Surgeon.*
B. F. ESHLFMAN, *Lt. Col. Comdg,*
W. M. OWEN, *Major,*
Lt. G. B. DERUSSY, *2nd Co.,*
Lt. H. A. BATTLES, *4th Co.,*
Capt. J. B RICHARDSON *2nd Co.,*
E. J. KURSHEEDT, Adjutant,
Capt. JOS. NORCOM *4th Co.,*
Capt. ANDREW HERO, JR., *3rd Co.,*
Lt. JNO. M. GALBRAITH, *1st Co.,*

Capt. EDWARD OWENS, *1st Co.*
W. H. WILKINS, *2nd Co.,*
W. H. ELLIS, *3rd Co.,*
JNO. B.GRETTER, *3rd Co.*
SAML. BLAND, *3rd Co.*
P. W. PETTISS, *3rd Co.*
P. O. FAZENDE, *1st Co.,*
VAN VINSON, *1st Co.*
JNO. R. MCGAUGHEY, *1st Co.*
A. G. KNIGHT, *2nd Co.,*
JNO. S. FISH, *4th Co.*

HEAD-QUARTERS BATTALION WASHINGTON
ARTILLERY,
Near Petersburg, Va., May 5th, 1864.

Gentlemen:--Agreeably to your very kind invitation
the manuscript of the Lecture to which you refer is
submitted to your disposal. A few slight but appropriate
changes have been made. Several paragrabs appear which
could not be delivered on the occasions of my public
discourse. I have quoted more perhaps than is usual in
productions of this kind; but I preferred that what I
believe to be the truth on some points should receive that
support which it may properly derive from the sanction of
weighty names. Please accept, gentlemen, my grateful
acknowlegments of the honor which has been done me in
this request.

I am, Gentlemen,
Very Respectfully,
Your Obedient Servant,

WM. A. HALL,
Chaplain, B. W. A.

To Dr. E. S. DREW, *Surg.; Lt. Col.* B. F. ESHLEMAN, *Comdg.; Maj.* W. M. OWEN, *Lt.* G. B. DE RUSSY, and others.

THE HISTORIC SIGNIFICANCE OF THE SOUTHERN REVOLUTION.

The Southern Revolution has been already discussed in various aspects, social, political, economic, through thought and blood. But we propose a distinct and wider view. We propose to inquire, what does this great revolution mean when considered as a movement in history? For that it deserves to be studied as a great historic movement, inferior to none preceding, is evident from its relations to the past, the present and the future. Let us ascertain, if possible, the real causes of this unprecedented struggle.

> "*Our siege of sorrow,*
> *Proportioned to its cause, no greater is*
> *Than that which makes it*"

What also is the great historic design of this Revolution? And what historic results will ensue from its successful issue? All of which we may now anticipate, though we may not be able to calculate the measure of their fulness. I would conduct this inquiry upon the idea that the meaning of any periodic or national life is to be ascertained by consulting the nature and the bearings of the philosophy, the inmost ideas, which make up and control that life. For human history, considered as to its matter, is a manifestation of the human mind; as to its outward, written form, it is a record of the action of that mind in all the directions in which it has wrought. Withal there is the double truth that God and man are the two great factors of history; both co-operating to accomplish the heavenly purpose; the One working with the independent free-agency proper to a self existent, independent Being; the other working with the dependent free-agency proper to a created and therefore dependent being; yet God all in all, working in and through and over man. History is therefore, in a higher sense, the manifestation of God in his providence; it is also a record of that divine providence. Prophecy is history yet to come, the God of providence yet unrevealed, untraced, ever adding to the canon of the providential scripture Without accepting the entire development theory of the German school, I believe that all historic ideas do beget and influence and modify each other; and control, through a sort of genetic development, the periodic and national lifes of history; so that each succeeding period of history is, so to speak, a development out of the preceding. Each gathers up the historic forces of the preceding, and adding new and modifying elements of its own passes on to the accomplishment of its appointed mission--the working out of the great principles which each embodies within itself.

Truly the prosecution of such an inquiry, involves no easy task. It demands that we divest ourselves of all that is temporary or special. We must rise above the present if we would reach the highest solution of our case. We must survey this great movement, not as politicians merely, not as religionists, not even as *Southrons*, but as thinkers, controlled by the noble spirit of the philosophy of history. It is no affected humility, but the simple truth to acknowledge, that I do not hope to prove equal to the high demands of this subject. But I would endeavor to establish from history itself *four* distinct propositions. *First*, that this Revolution marks the beginning of the last application of the great law by which all history is governed; *Secondly*, that it is a remarkable historic protest against philosophic infidelity and disorganizing wrong; *Thirdly*, that it aims to conserve the perfection of republican government, and therein to vindicate the organic law under which civil government was first constituted by God; *Fourthly*, that it marks the beginning of what would seem to be the last period of human history on its present conditions. I therefore solicit your kind attention while I endeavor to present in this form, as briefly as possible, what I take to be the answer to this earnest question,--*What is the Historic Significance of the Southern Revolution?*

    I. This Revolution has a grand significance, in that *it marks the beginning of the last application of the great law by which all history is governed*. The history of our race properly starts from that event known as the Fall. Viewed from a secular stand-point it is amenable to this historic law that-- *power seeks an equilibrium*. Hence power is constantly tending from the *individual* to the *mass*--by *mass* I mean a consolidated despotism of physical force--and from the *mass* back to the *individual*. Moreover this history seems to be logically divisible thus far, on this idea of power, into *five distinct periods*; each governed by one characteristic principle, The *First Period* of history we may describe as the *Period of Formation*; it extends from the Fall of man to the rise of the earliest of the Ancient Empires. The *Second Period* is the *Period of Conquest*; extending from the rise of that Empire to about 100 B. C. when Julius Caesar began that career of Conquest which ended in the culmination of the Roman Empire The *Third Period* is the *Period of Consolidation*; extending from the opening of Cæsar's career to the downfall of the Roman Empire in A. D. 476. The *Fourth Period* is the *Period of Disintegration*, accompanied by the *predominance of the church*; extending from the downfall of the Roman Empire to the rise of the Reformation in Europe in 1516. The *Fifth Period* is the *Period of Reformation*, or of *Individual Freedom*; extending from the rise of the Reformation in Europe to the year 1860, as it seems to me. Then we would seem to have the *Sixth*, and, as it would appear, the last period of history on its present conditions, the *Period of Conservatism*. On this we would seem to have just entered, and the South, unconsciously to herself does seem to have led the way. Let us now trace, as rapidly as possible, through these periods, the application of this law of power; and please to observe the distinction that while there are six periods of history, there are but *three* movements of power.

In the *Period of Formation* man appears before us first as an *individual*. All the essential elements of the Primeval Constitution pass over into this period, but all radically modified by two new ideas, Sin and Redemption. These are the two fundamental conditions of human history which underlie and pervade the providential government of God through the whole administration of the economy of grace. The law of love being dethroned in the human breast, that of selfishness reigns. Man seeks his own irrespective of all else. Especially does he aim at the possession of unchecked *power*; first, perhaps, for self-protection and then for advantage over his fellows. Owing partly to physical causes and chiefly to the collective force of this law of power, man undergoes a sort of *formative process*; he passes out of his individual posture, through the family, into larger associations, until finally great and powerful communities rise before us.

This introduces the *Second Period* of History, the *Period of Conquest*. The idea of selfish power passes over into this period; but it is no longer the power of man the individual, or of man in smaller associations, but of man in large and powerful communities, swaying the besom of *aggregate power*, chiefly for the *conquest* of his fellows. Each of these Empires lives its allotted time and, after achieving its historic mission, gives way to another more mighty and imposing. This period ends in the bosom of the Roman life, about 100 B. C., when Julius Cæsar began that remarkable career of Conquest which ended in the Culmination of the Roman Empire.

At this point we mark the beginning of the *Third Period*, the *Period of Consolidation*; extending from the opening of Cæsar's career to the Downfall of the Roman Empire in 476. The Roman Empire, the last and grandest of the old-world powers, embraces all the civilized world. Having reached apparently the utmost limits of conquest, having even satiated the demands of an almost superhuman ambition, the imperial Mistress of the Earth labors to *consolidate* all the peoples and elements of the age beneath her own control. This era is grandly featured by the sum of old-world's life--by the highest development of law and government and social civilization in the Roman State; by the highest æsthetic and intellectual culture in Greece; by the transition of that culture to the Roman mind; by the Incarnation of the Son of God, in which God over man becomes God in man, and the idea of Redemption is completed for its work; by the passing over of a pure Theism from the Hebrew nation to the christian church; by the perfection and universal spread of the Greek language as the vernacular in order to its being the organ of a more profound and spiritual statement of religious truth; and by the establishment of a vast system of military roads and lines of intercommunication, extending from Rome as the centre throughout this consolidated world; all concentrated and, as it were absorbed, by this great *consolidating* power; and all conducing to the most fruitful event of this era, the universal spread of the Gospel through the evangelistic agencies of the christian church. But the time has now come for another great historic movement. The Old-world has done its work; it has exhausted all of its historic forces. These having reached their utmost limit, they begin to produce only evil fruits which appear in the fearful corruptions of the day. Not even the church of God escapes the contamination. The law of selfishness, the love of power, returns to punish itself. A new and more vigorous element must be added to the decaying energies of the Old-world's life in order to conserve and perpetuate religion and civilization through out the world. The decree uttered by the Roman Senate against Carthage rebounds upon the cruel Empire-- *Delenda Roma.* And now the Northern Tribes, the great Teutonic or German element, rush down upon Italy, the Imperial Seat of the Cæsars, beautiful even in her corruption, majestic even in her weakness, and, as the rod of Jehovah, dash her in pieces like a potter's vessel. The field of history is strewn with the fragments of a magnificent Empire, and the light of liberty, long dimly burning, seems to be entombed forever in the darkness of the Middle Ages.

The Fall of the Roman Empire not only marks the close of the Third Period of history and the opening of the *Fourth*, but it marks the close of Ancient history with all that distinguishes it from that which we term Modern history. The essential characteristics of the latter as distinguished from the former are the addition of this

Teutonic or German element to the previous historic forces, and the *consequent* recession of power from the *mass* to the *individual*. During this period all pre-existing political bodies and relations are broken up, *disintegrated*. Chaotic ruin threatens all that is precious to society. But, as the only institution that could survive the crash of dynasties and the collision of newly combining elements, the Roman church controls the storm. Within her bosom, as the only refuge, gather the elements that are to civilize the world to come. All the corruptions of the previous era, which adhere by an almost physical affinity; all its æsthetic and intellectual culture; its grandly developed law and science of government; its administrative skill and ability; and strange to say, this gigantic idea of consolidated, imperial power, which was wrought upon the church by Hildebrand as it had been wrought upon the state by the Cæsars--all pass over into the bosom of the christian church. There they are indeed preserved, but almost at the expense of her religious life. This period is, therefore, strongly marked by the *predominance of the church*. It is in this respect the opposite of the preceding era; in which the political predominated over the religious element, except during a brief transition-epoch when church and state were in alliance under Constantine the Great. Its life was a vast church-life All of its intellectual energies were expended upon the various topics of theology, under the guidance of the Aristotelian philosophy, in the unavoidable though misdirected effort to mediate between reason and revelation, to reconcile faith and knowledge; and, therefore, as a means to this end, to give a logical statement and consistency to the truths of revealed religion. That whole series of efforts has been described by the term *Scholasticism*; which, being necessarily confined to the church and thus to the universities which were controlled by the church, was the only form in which the intellectual life of that age could utter itself. In the almost exact language of a living German writer;--the whole Scholastic Theology became divided into two schools--"the one exalting the understanding, the other the will as its highest principle; both being driven into essentially differing directions by this opposition of a theoretical and a practical principle. Even with this began the downfall of Scholasticism." Although while, standing wholly in the service of the church, it had nevertheless grown out of a scientific impulse and so naturally awakened a spirit of inquiry and a sense of knowledge; although it made the objects of faith the objects of thought; though it raised men from the sphere of unconditional faith to that of doubt, of investigation, and of knowledge, and by its very effort to demonstrate the principles of theology established, though against its knowledge and design, the authority of reason; although it introduced to the world another principle than that of the old church, the principle of the thinking spirit, or at least prepared the way for the victory of that principle; though even its deformities--the many absurd questions upon which the Schoolmen divided, their thousand-fold unnecessary and accidental distinctions, their inquisitiveness and subtleties--all grew out of a spirit of investigation which could utter itself only in this way under the all-powerful ecclesiastical spirit of the time,--still this highest point of Scholasticism was the turning point to its self-destruction. The reasonableness of revealed truth, "the oneness of faith and knoweldge, had always been the fundamental premise of the Schoolmen; but this premise fell away, and the whole basis of their philosophy was given up in principle the moment Duns Scotus placed the problem of theology in the practical When the practical and the theoretical became divided, philosophy broke loose from theology and knowledge from faith; the great principles of Scholasticism came to an end; knowledge assumed a position apart from faith and above authority - this gave birth to modern philosophy--and the religious consciousness broke loose from the traditional dogma-- this begat the Reformation."[1] Thus this period carries through the Roman church the same effort to wield the sceptre of consolidated power; but by the very nature of its inward, intellectual life, it breaks down upon the Sixteenth Century in precisely analogous results.

Those results brightly define the beginning of the *Fifth Period* of history, that wonderful protest of religion

----

[1] Schwegler's History of Philosophy, Transition to Mod. Phil.

and of thought, which asserted itself early in the Sixteenth Century in the German Reformation, That period closed, it seems to me, in the year 1860, when the rise of the Southern Revolution announced the opening of the *Sixth*, and, as it would appear, the last period of human history on its present conditions.

"All the elements of the new era, the struggle against Scholasticism, the advancement of the natural sciences, the revival of letters and the more enlarged culture thus secured, the striving after national independence, the attempts of the State to free itself from the church and the hierarchy, and above all the desire of the thinking spirit for freedom from the fetters of authority--all these elements found their focus and point of union in the German Reformation. Though having its root, at first, in practical and religious and national interests, and expending itself mainly upon the christian doctrine and the church, yet was the Reformation, in principle and in its true consequences, a rupture of the thinking spirit with authority, a protesting against the fetters of the positive. The purely human as such, the individual heart and conscience, the subjective conviction, in a word, the rights of the subject now began to be of worth. In the same way on the side of knowledge the individual man came back to himself and threw off the restraints of authority. He was impressed with the conviction that the whole process of Redemption must be experienced within himself, that his reconciliation to God and salvation was his own concern for which he needed no mediation of clergy. He found his whole being in his faith, in the depths of his feelings and convictions. For religion reduced to its simplest elements will be found its have its source, like philosophy, in the self-knowledge of the reason."[2]

And yet religion, unlike philosophy, is the growth of a soul, a loving reason, renewed, empowered and taught by the Holy Ghost. Thus we perceive that the leading principle of this era was *freedom of individual thought*; this was the chief historic force that generated and controlled its grand and fruitful life. Its work now done, that period has detached itself from the present and put on the robes of a kingly past.

It is also clear that Ancient History, taken as a whole, was a movement of power from the *individual* to the *mass*; reaching its highest development when power *massed* itself in the massive Roman State. On the other hand Modern History has been a recession of power from the *mass* to the *individual*. The era of the Middle Ages did, indeed, carry the same effort at consolidated power in

_____

[2] Dr. Schwegler.

another direction, namely through the Roman church; but all along that very effort, moving in that direction, power was descending to the individual; because religion, which is the soul of the church, works upon the most individual of all man's relations, those which he sustains to God. That tendency has been moving from the bosom of Scholasticism within the Roman church, but more especially of the Sixteenth Century, to the present day. Perverted in part, as we shall see, into modern philosophical atheism, it reached its extreme development in the Northern portion of the late United States. Against this we are now contending. It is also true that in both these cycles, Ancient and Modern, we discover many lesser movements, actions and reactions; but these, like the billows on the Gulf Stream, or the eddying currents of the Mississippi, are either lesser applications of the same great law or of collateral and connected principles; they all move on in the same general direction in obedience to the same great law. Now the movement which power has already begun is the last which it can possibly make. Let it be observed that history on its *sacred* side is, likewise, susceptible of a threefold division. In the ancient dispensation God the Father, God absolutely considered, was more singly revealed. During the time of the Incarnation God the Son, to whom was committed all power in heaven and earth, was more specially revealed; and that upon the summit of the consolidated Roman Empire which gathered together the very energies that were to aid the universal spread of His Gospel. The Day of Pentecost began the more special revelation of God the Holy Ghost, the Third Person of the Trinity, operating most fully upon the *individual* man in the most individual of all his relations. So likewise on the one side of power-- and, it would seem, by virtue of the inward connecting principles of the Divine economy,--Ancient history was a movement of power from the individual to the mass; Modern history has been a recession of power from the mass to the individual. The reaction from the extreme of individual authority which has now begun, cannot result again in the mass, because the God of History never repeats himself in such great movements, conducted as they are, upon those inward, connecting principles. History seems to have reached on the side of power a place analogous to that which it has reached on the side of redemption, that is, the dispensation of the Holy Ghost operating most intensely on the individual man in the most individual of all his relations those which he sustains to God. The last days of this dispensation are yet to be completed "Then cometh the end, when the Son shall deliver up the kingdom of God, even the Father; when he shall have put down all rule and all authority, and power. Then shall the Son also himself be subject to him that put all things under him, that God may be all in all."[3] The idea of God in his tri-personality will pass back

---

[3] 1 Cor. xv:24,28.

into that of God in his unity; the dispensations of God, in the Trinity, will have passed back into that of God in his unity. Power must, therefore, settle on a point where it will find its *equilibrium*, between the despotism of the individual and the despotism of the mass. This is last and the only movement which it can make; and this will complete the trinity of historic developments.

II. This Revolution has a profound significance in that *it is a great historic protest, the only one of the sort in history, against philosophic infidelity and disorganizing wrong*. We are combatting a fanaticism, without foundation in the Bible or in philosophy, which assails all the fundamental principles of human and of divine nature, as they are revealed in the Word and expounded in the providence of God; as they are embodied in the worthy social, political and religious systems of the present day. Previous history discovers no such assault, so profound, so comprehensive. The French Revolution, the final fruit of materialism, moved more upon the surface; it ran its course with French vivacity through the ghastly reign of terror. But this crusade lays hold with *ideal* strength upon the age-laid pillars of society. The fruit of the extremest individualism, it is the most fearful illustration in history of the truth--that the intellectual and moral philosophy of a people, which educate their heart and conscience and intellect, determine their whole inward and outward life, their character form of government, of society, and of religion--and decide their destiny.

We may rest assured that this war is not designed to abolish or to injure slavery. It may be intended to produce in us a willingness to part with the institution when God's time shall have come, if ever it does come. But no further can it aim, unless the Almighty is working, contrary to the analogy of all his past dealings with our race, to carry out an ultimate purpose affecting deeply the interests of his creatures, without giving them the slightest indication of such design. For touching the question of slavery in its moral bearings, this revolution clearly aims to vindicate the word of God, which approves that institution and the providence of God, which has wisely preserved it. Stated essentially in the primeval law of nature; restated under the Covenant of Grace, with modifications suited to a condition of mixed good and evil; sanctified and regulated by statement and by precept throughout the word of God, which puts the relation of master and slave, as one of the four essential relations of the household; pervading the basis and the structure of the whole economy of Redemption through its earthly stage; standing under the eye of Jehovah in the patriarchal era, the first period of history, and reappearing, in the identical system of these States in this last period; upheld and illustrated, for the wisest purposes, by the providence of God throughout the entire history of our race; and now assailed in this last period of history by the combined infidelity of the ages--the doctrine of domestic slavery and the system of labor which time has built upon it are in a true sense divine; they are the sum and the condition of the African's welfare; and they will probably continue on

some part of earth until the last day, when the economy of grace will demit whatsoever is peculiar to its earthly stage and passover its enduring glories on the Lamb's Book of Life.[4] Has not this Revolution already done what no other instrumentality could have effected? Confronting, as we do, the only case in history of a senseless fanaticism controlling most of the leading minds in christendom, what, upon the analogies of history, could be expected to break the grasp of such a fanaticism, except just such a revolution? This war has set the seal of providence before the eyes of the world upon the stability of domestic slavery and of Southern Society; it has refuted the slanders of our enemies upon the character of the Southern people; it has torn off the silver veil from the face of Northern character and revealed to a disgusted world the hideous features of the false Prophet. With all reverence I believe that we have come too far in civilization, that we are too near the latter day glory, for a godless fanaticism to master and desolate the church of the living God, and put back that civilization several

––––––––––––––––

[4] Gen. 2: 5, 8, 20-9: 25-27. Ex. 20: 19, 17. Ps. 40: 6 with Ex. 21: 6 and Heb. 10: 6, 7, 10. Phil. 2: 7. Rom. 6: 14, 16, 22. Rev. 19: 18.

hundred years. Above all, it is this that lends an awful sacredness this contest on our part--that the rightful claims of Jehovah are deeply involved. Grand as the contest is "for independence and liberty, for the altars and the graves of our fathers, and for the more sacred rights of conscience and freedom to worship God, it rises to the moral sublime" when we consider that we are permitted to vindicate the supremacy of Jehovah's word and the purity of his government. This explains why the Southern Clergy, standing aside for the time from all their previous practice, have shown such an active sympathy with this political revolution. "It is not only from the impulse of a lofty patriotism, grand as that sentiment may be; but out of loyalty to God against whose rightful supremacy a wicked infidelity has lifted its rebellious arm. Of all men they are best qualified to appreciate the moral bearings of this controversy. Much as they desire their country to be free, with an infinitely deeper fervor do they desire that God should reign."[5]

Let nothing in this statement imply the least condemnation of anything that was true in the Reformation era--that noble *protest of individual freedom*.

---

[5] Rev. B. M. PALMER, D. D., of New Orleans--Discourse before the Legislature of Georgia, March 27th, 1863.

Never can we too highly estimate the value of that great intellectual and moral movement. It has conferred upon us all the glory and blessedness of modern civilization and religion. We simply discover that, as in former ages so in this, men have acted upon the fallacy that the reverse of wrong as such is right. Protestantism did spring out of the same essence that begat modern philosophy; and in their subsequent progress the two have gone hand in hand together. But as the deathly Upas flourishes on the richest soil, so have false philosophies, bearing the deadliest fruits, grown up on the soil that bears the true. Out of that very movement was dragged a needless tendency, whose results have culminated in the fearful crusade that clothes the South in mourning to-day. Nearly all the world-life at the present day--and especially this American war--may be traced largely and directly to these causes--the Transcendental Philosophy of Germany--the atheistic philosophy of the later and earlier French School--and the selfish utilitarian Moral Philosophy of Dr PALEY, a divine of the church of England, It is eminently true that the Northern mind, by its education during the last seventy years under these false philosophies, has been prepared for this inhuman crusade upon the existence of the Southern States. Let us trace the process, and in order to its clearer comprehension let us define in passing, the nature of philosophy, and the aim of mordern philosophy.

Philosophy is a science distinct in itself. The science, commonly so called, get the material of truth from observation--"they find it at hand and take up just as they find it. Philosophy, on the other hand, is never satisfied with receiving that which is given simply as it is given, but rather follows it out to its ultimate grounds; it examines every individual thing with reference to a final principle and considers it one link in the whole chain of thought." Philosophy, therefore, is the science of final principles--of ultimate ideas. Scrutinizing the material and the spiritual world--the world of mind and the outward world of varied life and manifold relations divine and human, it seeks to understand these, and to refer their glorious facts to some ultimate principles by which they may be bound together and classified. Hence philosophy is inseparable from man as a thinking being; and, as Mr. PEARSON well remarks[*][6]--"the rise of speculative philosophy in any age or country where there are thinkers seems inevitable. It is the natural consequence of the mind's desire to penetrate into the mysteries of existence and to know all things. Man himself is a mystery, the world around him is a mystery, the great God above him is a mystery, and the relations between each and all of these are profoundly and impressively mysterious. And while the great majority of men are content with the knowledge that lies upon the surface of things, there are those who must endeavor to get beyond and solve the

—————————————

[6] Infidelity, p.352.

problems of mysterious existence. This, in itself, is not to be regarded as an evil. It indicates a reflecting age and marks the advancement of a community in mental culture. The evil is, when it spurns the investigation of palpable facts and indubitable evidence, treats as empirical the honest method of induction, and passing the bounds of all fair and legitimate inquiry," transcends the proper limits of human thought.

Now it has been the aim of modern philosophy, with perhaps larger success, to ascertain the final principles of all truth. Especially has it labored in the sphere of mental science. There it has raised this fundamental inquiry-- what is the origin of our knowledge? We seem to derive our impressions of the external world through the senses. But is the mind simply *a blank sheet* upon which those impressions are stamped? Or does it essentially modify them? Or does the mind contain within itself the *types* of the world without, certain innate ideas, which are only aroused into activity--whenever we behold the external world? Briefly, does our knowledge originate in the senses, or within the mind itself, or is it a sort of compromise between the workings of both thought and sense--of reflection and sensation? Now precisely as men have given undue prominence to the *ideal*, or the *sensational* origin of knowledge, in that proportion have they developed a philosophy grossly material, and sensual, or vaguely ideal, and transcendental. Such, precisely, have been the painful and needless developments in two branches of modern philosophy.

Beneath their united effects we are staggering today. Mr. Locke announced with much truth, that our knowledge is the combined result of sensation and reflection. Mr. Hobbes, seizing upon the purely material side of this theory, made knowledge to be simply transformed sensations. Others resolved the soul itself into a mere collection of atoms--a material substance; thus overturning the doctrine of the immortality of the soul, with its consequent religion and morality. From these, Condillac in France, Diderot, D'Holbach, and the *Systems de la Nature*, carried materialism to its bitterest fruits in that beautiful land of the vine. Starting with the idea that knowledge originates wholly in the senses, this philosophy soon identified man with material nature, made death an eternal sleep, piety the superstition of the senseless, and morality the religion of the fool. Absorbing the Deity in his own creation, it declared that God was the universe. At last, seizing with Celtic frenzy, and yet with sensual weakness, upon the very foundations of society, as it had upon the throne of Jehovah, it enthroned the Goddess of material reason and rioted through the terrible reign of 1793. On one side we are now combatting the last results of that atheism. The theory of "human rights," which Thos. Paine sowed deeply over the receptive North, after the first Revolution, was derived from the French atheism. And the very text upon which this Abolition crusade is discoursing so bloodily the dogma, that "all men are created free, and have equal rights to liberty," was incorporated into the Declaration of

Independence by Mr. Jefferson, a Southern statesman, who imbibed his philosophical sentiments from the schools of France.

The German philosophy has been a reaction on the side of idealism, against the French extreme. Starting from the principle of Des Cartes, that philosophy, or the pursuit of knowledge, should be begun with universal doubt, it moved through the phases of Leibnitz and Wolf, until it reached the extreme development in the transcendental Pantheism of the later German School. Finding the origin of knowledge wholly in the soul of man, this makes him the centre and the solution of the universe. Proclaiming that the universe is God, it destroys the distinct personality of Jehovah. Man being a part of the universe, is therefore a part of God; he is to himself the only God; and the only Divine revelation that is or can be made to him, is the intuition of his own conciousness. Being thus intensely individual, making each man the sole criterion to himself of all truth, this philosophy transcends every proper limit of human thought; it refuses obedience to any outward revelation from a personal God; it denies every claim of an historic Christ, or an evidential Christianity; it overrides every restraint or obligation, social or political; and aims to adjust the universe, things human and divine, upon the intuitions of this exalted man--God, the self-constituted judge of all things. Pantheism has just completed its ideal course and work. According to the best historians of the German philosophy, that philosophy is entering upon a new phase, which is as yet undetermined. One of the most remarkable facts of the age is, that STRAUSS, who made the famous attempt in his *Life of Jesus*, on this transcendental theory, to make the historic Christ a mere idea, begotten in the consciousness of humanity, a mere Christian myth, and the Gospel history a mere spiritual mythology, has just recanted his entire theory; thus verifying the beautiful remark of Isaac Taylor,--the moment you prove the resurrection of Jesus from the dead, the whole fabric of modern infidelity falls to the ground.

But above all other causes, the intensely practical effects of that Pantheism are upon us to-day. This whole Northern crusade is the special effect in this country of the ideal atheism of the German School, precisely as the Revolution of 1793, was the effect in France of the material atheism of the French School. It has appeared here because the conditions of American life, unlike those of despotic Europe, were highly favorable to its extremest development, The French Revolution was more superficial, special, Celtic; this crusade is more profound comprehensive, Teutonic; the latter has been slower in its development, than the former, because the ideal moves more slowly than the material. It has been already said that the moral philosophy of DR. PALEY, has had an influence in forming the present condition of the Northern mind. JOHN RANDOLPH once observed that New England derived her morality from Dr. Paley and the Jesuits. Defining virtue to be that which conduces to one's own happiness, rather than conformity to the outwardly revealed will of God, Dr. Paley's philosophy has educated the Northern heart and conscience in selfishness, while German Transcendentalism has been in like manner educating the Northern intellect, until the bulk of Northern life has become a monstrous Egoism. Imported during the last eighty years, In the works of German philosophers and in the writings of M. VICTOR COUSINS, the brilliant Lecturer before the University of Paris, this German Pantheism has transformed almost all the educated mind of the North. It has pervaded every sphere of life, every rank of society, and every department of thought. It has given birth to almost every *ism* that afflicts that people; and these all, representing in their varied forms the sum of modern infidelity, have found their focus and point of union in Abolitionism. The lost and lawless spirit of the ages, up from the vasty deep of error--this has been animating the year-long crusade upon the Southern States. It declared through MR, BURLINGAME, some years ago, on the floor of the United States Congress,--"The times demand and we must have an anti-slavery Constitution, an anti-slavery Bible, and an anti-slavery God!" Transcendentalism in politics! Extermination to God! It declared through MR. SEWARD, before the Buffalo Convention of 1855,-- "Slavery must and can be abolished. You and I can and must do it. It may bring about a struggle which will subvert this constitution; but slave-holders shall perish in the struggle!" Rebellion against the government! Extermination to the whites! It declared through MR.

SEWARD again, before the Chicago Convention of 1860,--"There are the Southern States, with the finest territory on the face of the earth, peopled by four millions of blacks. That territory is wanted for the free white men of the North; those blacks must be put out of the way! " Extermination to the blacks ! It declared through the Reverend BEECHER, a few years ago, when lifting from a desecrated pulpit, the word of God, he exclaimed, "If the God of that Bible be the God of slavery, I would help dethrone Him from the universe!" Transcendentalism in the pulpit! As faithless as the arch-deceiver, more merciless than the grave; choosing, rather like Milton's Satan, "to reign in hell than serve in heaven;" it has spoken through an Abolition press; it has declaimed from Abolition rostrums it has deceived through Abolition Statesmen; it has destroyed through menial armies; it did "subvert the Constitution," in the election of Mr Lincoln for the perdition of slave-holders--the great Republic is no more! Some noble spirits tried to avert the catastrophe which they saw approaching. The great WEBSTER, a type far more of what is true than of what was false in New England, turned first in one direction and then in another, but with evident hope to the generous Southerner. On one occasion in 1850, he said to an eminent gentleman from Maryland,[7]--"Sir, I think it my

---

[7] This conversation has never before been published. It was related to me some weeks ago, by the son of the

duty to say some things to you and other gentlemen from
the South, of like position and character. In my opinion, a
crisis is at hand in the history of the country. The mass of
the Northern people have been thoroughly educated in
Abolitionism. It is preached from the pulpit, it pours from
the press, it is taught in the schools, it is imbibed at the
mother's breast. The feeling is with them a religious
sentiment; and, sir, the day is near, when they will as one
man demand of the South the abolition of slavery. Now,
sir, I beg that you, and gentlmen of like influence, will go
among your people, and persuade them to acquiesce in
that demand; for, sir if it is not peaceably met, the country
is ruined!" "Mr. Webster," replied the gentleman, "I am
both surprised and grieved to hear such sentiments from
you. I can only say to you, from what I know of the
character of the Southern people, if that demand ever is
made, the sword will be drawn, and that will decide the
issue." On another occasion that noble statesman poured
out the indignation of his agonized soul, on the destroyers
of his country in this language,--"If these infernal
abolitionists once succeed in grasping the powers of
government, they will overturn the Constitution, trample
on all law, destroy every vested right, lay violent hands
on all who oppose them, and overwhelm the country in
irretrievable ruin." Alas! that the tearful prophecy must

---

gentleman referred to, now an officer of the Confederate
Government; and I have taken the liberty to insert it here.

needs have been fulfilled. Alas! that iniquity could have power to destroy such a hopeful national life. The golden tongue of liberty is sealed., and unless the South be faithful, is sealed up in silence forever!

> "The chord, the harp's full chord is hushed;
> The voice hath died away,
> Whence music, like sweet waters, gushed
> But yesterday."

It is evident from this discussion, that the question of African slavery is not fundamental to this revolution, except so far as it involves the doctrine of the providential inferiority of the African race. That institution is not a *cause* of this war, but simply an *occasion* of it. It is only the *object* against which the radicalism of the North has arrayed itself in Abolitionism. Had not this object existed, that Dragon from the bottomless pit, would have discovered some other eminence of Southern life, on which to expend its fury.

There is one other topic to which I must refer, not only to preserve the unity of this discussion, but to enter my dissent from certain impressions which have been urgently diffused in public and private, by mouth and pen. So far as I am aware, there has been but one prominent exception to this general procedure. During the debate in the Confederate Congress respecting the adoption of our national motto, *Deo vindice,* a distinguished Senator from

Louisiana uttered a brief but able dissent from the clamor which I am about to oppose. It is proper, as well as necessary, for me to remark, what indeed, this argument has already established, that *Puritanism properly so called, has no connection whatsoever, with this inhuman crusade upon the Confederate States.* With all due respect to those who think differently, I must confess my amazement at the persistency with which some have bruited the absurd idea, that this unprecedented struggle-- the anomaly of all history--is a renewal of the strife between the Puritan and the Cavalier! And I know not how to account for this singular phenomenon, unless it may be ascribed to ignorance or to passion. I say, *to ignorance or to passion*; for surely there are none among us who would have this to be the price of our incalculable sufferings--a condition of society in church and state, that shall inure to the special benefit of certain mythical individuals styled Cavaliers and their descendants or adherents! If so, the Southern people will repudiate an issue for which they are ignorantly sacrificing their all. Who are these Cavaliers? Where have they ever been in any considerable numbers upon this continent? Call up the men who composed the Virginia Convention of 1776, and ask them from what stock they came, by birth and training, and by election. Were they Cavaliers in blood or in principle? Almost without exception, their descent was Huguenot, Scotch and Irish.

"O! that the history of such a race were worthily written. O! that our historians, instead of beginning and ending with the acts of the beggarly governors, who for a century and a half, were sent over to fatten on the revenues of the Colony, and calling such a record, Virginia's history, had looked to the races from which this glorious stock had risen, their high spirit, their burning patriotism! These writers tell us that these noble qualities have been derived from a class of men who came over from time to time, few and far between, and under the name of Cavaliers, sought a livelihood in the Colony. Miserable figment! Outrageous calumny! Why, sir, the Cavalier was essentially a slave--a compound slave--a slave to the king and a slave to the church. He was the last man in the world from whom any great elemental principle of liberty and law could come. He was as incapable of transmitting such a principle to others, as he was of conceiving it himself. It is true that some of this class did come over at intervals. Some came with the gallant JOHN SMITH; but when he found out how worthless they were, he implored the Virginia Company to send no more. Even the gallant SMITH himself, left the colony after a short sojourn, and was soon followed by PERCY, whom the first honors of the Colony could not tempt to remain within its borders. But when the great gold shipment turned to dross, the Cavalier came no more. A home in the wilderness, to be cleared by his own axe, and guarded by his own musket, against a wily foe, was no place for the voluptuary and the idler.--Sir, I look with contempt on that miserable figment which has so long held a place in our histories, and which seeks to trace

the distinguishing and salient points of the Virginia
character, to the influence of those butterflies of the
British aristocracy, who, unable to earn their bread at
home, came over to the Colony to feed on whatever
crumbs they might gather in some petty office, or from
the race-course, or from the gaming table, instead of
regarding those distinctive traits as the legitimate results
of a great Anglo-Saxon people, placed in a position of all
others, best adapted to the full and generous development
of their peculiar virtues. The secret of our colonial history
lies far deeper. If you will look back into the reigns of
Henry the Eighth and Elizabeth, you will find some of the
causes which led to the settlement of Virginia.--Still there
was in the Colony, a distinct Cavalier class, not wholly
contemptible in numbers, but more potent in influence,
which partook of the character that marked the foreign
original, and which in its modes of life, imitated English
manners, practiced English sports, cherished English
prejudices, and were proud of the glory of England, not in
its loftiest development but as casting its brightness, of all
others in the Colony, on itself, But even to this class,
some, who could trace a legitimate descent from those
who came over after the discomfiture and death of
Charles, did not belong. Their descendants differed
materially from their ancestors. The architects of their
own fortune, reared in that noblest of all schools, the
school of poverty, they had mingled freely with the
people, and shared their pursuits; and thus not only lost
their hereditary prejudices, but adopted popular views,

and became the most strenuous supporters of the very principles from which their ancestors would have recoiled. It was the spirit of Anglo Saxon liberty, inculcated for generations, by the peculiar circumstances of the Colony in their race, that made the names of Washington, George Mason and the Lees, a bulwark in the cause of independence. *But neither of these was the representative of the party to which, by the accident of birth he belonged.*--How that Convention would have laughed to scorn the notion that they, and those who chose them, owed their high courage, their keen sense of wrong, their exalted love of liberty in church and state, to a set of vagrants and office holders, who never drew a sword but in defence of a tyrant king, and whose highest ambition sought only the petty honors which a tyrant deemed high enough for his tools in a distant Colony! Pure and devoted patriots! they knew full well that their love of liberty, their hatred of wrong, their unflinching courage, came from another quarter. Whatever merits their fathers, or their fathers' fathers possessed, were all their own--And let me say to you, sir, how much more noble it is, as well as more true, how much more congenial to the pride and honor of the Virginian, to reflect that the virtues of his fathers are to be traced, not to a race of men whose whole career was one long, bitter and bloody protest against civil and religious freedom; but to the great Anglo-Saxon family, whose swords were never drawn in vain, and before whom the hosts of the Cavalier in the old world, were driven as chaff before the wind!--Such were the men, who in the council and in the field, achieved the Revolution. So far from the Cavalier influence bringing about the Revolution, the Revolution was brought about in spite of the Cavalier. The three greatest test measures of that epoch, were the resolutions of Henry, in 1765, against the stamp act; the resolutions of the same individual in the Convention of March, 1775, for putting the Colony into military array; and the resolution instructing the delegates in Congress to propose independence. Of all these measures the Cavalier party, as a party, was the stoutest opponent."[8]

———————————

[8] THE VIRGINIA CONVENTION OF 1776.--A discourse delivered before the Virginia Alpha of the Phi Beta Kappa Society, in the chapel of William and Mary College, in the city of Williamsburg, on the afternoon of July 3rd, 1855, by HUGH BLAIR GRIGSBY. Published by a resolution of the Society."--In this discourse this accomplished gentlemen shows that the original stock of Virginia was mostly Huguenot, German, Scotch and Irish; that the Cavalier element was small in her colonial era; that most of that class proved utterly "worthless;" and that the worthy but distinct Cavalier class who did contribute to the power of Southern life, gained influence only by adopting popular views, and by supporting the very principles from which their ancestors would have recoiled. These points Mr. Grigsby proves by references to historical documents and to the law-suit history of the

Clearly the vast majority of the first and later settlers in Virginia and the Southern Colonies, were not Cavaliers; and the immense majority of the present population of these States, are of any but Cavalier origin. The large majority of the settlers in the Northern Colonies, were not Puritans; and the vast majority of the present Northern population, are of any but Puritan origin. It has been estimated that *twelve millions* of the present population of twenty millions in the United States, are foreigners, and their immediate descendants, the worst elements chiefly of European society; and of the remaining eight millions, but a small portion are of Puritan descent, and a still smaller portion of any Puritan faith. Let it be remembered that this contest is of the whole South against the whole North; I mean all the representative elements of the one, against all the representative elements of the other.

Who were the Puritans? The term Puritan, had a threefold application with reference to morals, doctrine and politics. In the almost exact language of MR. NEAL, the acknowledged standard authority upon this subject, this term came to be applied as an epithet, first in

---

colonial era, and by indicating the history of some of the leading families of Virginia, the names of whose founders he cites.--*See Discourse, especially pp.* 36-44. The italics are mine.

England, in the year 1564, when it was urged upon the clergy of the several dioceses to subscribe to the ceremonies, liturgy and discipline of the Established Church, precisely as they then existed; those who refused were called *Puritans*, a name of reproach, derived from the Cathari or Puritani of the third century after Christ; though correct enough to signify their desires for what they deemed a purer form of religious worship. When the doctrines of Arminius took place in the latter end of the reign of James I, those who adhered to Calvin's explanation of the five disputed points--a part of which was embodied in the Seventeenth Article of the noble creed of the Church of England--were called *Doctrinal Puritans*. "At length, says MR. FULLER, the name was improved, to stigmatize all those who endeavored in their devotions to accompany the minister with a pure heart, and were unusually pure in their lives. Queen Elizabeth, having conceived a strong aversion to these people, turned all her artillery against them; for, besides the ordinary court of the bishops, her majesty appointed a new tribunal, called the Court of High Commissions, which suspended and deprived men of their livings, not by the verdict of twelve men upon oath, but by the sovereign determination of three commissioners of her majesty's own nomination--their sentence founded not upon the statute laws of the realm, but upon the bottomless deep of the canon law; and instead of producing witnesses in open court to prove the charge, they assumed the power of *administering an oath, ex officio*, whereby the prisoner was obliged to answer all questions put to him, though never so prejudicial to his own defence; if he refused to swear, he was imprisoned for contempt; and if he took the oath, he was convicted upon his own confession![9] All who opposed this mode of procedure were called *Puritans*. The Puritans, therefore, included all the lovers of civil and religious liberty in that age, but especially in the English Church and State. Doubtless, there were extremists among them, as there have always been among all parties. After the Restoration, many of them came to be known as Independents; and to these, especially in America, the name Puritans, has been adroitly confined; some of them came to be known as Baptists; some as Presbyterians; many of them were Episcopalians, among the brighest ornaments of the Church of England, some of whom were leaders even in the long Parliament though they did not all separate from the Established Church; and some of these Puritans were men of no religious persuasion, who opposed the prevailing ideas in Church and State, purely on political grounds. Especially, was this epithet *Puritan*, flung at those who advocated purity of life in opposition to the disgusting immoralities of the age; the epithet *Cavalier*, was hurled with equal vehemence at the other side. The extremes of these parties, on this idea, were

---

[9] *History of the Puritans, Preface, p.* 10

extremes of English character in two opposite directions; the one was *licentiousness*, the other *asceticism*; both untrue and reprehensible.

What, then, was Puritanism? It was the protest of a large and influential portion of the Established Church of England, against what they deemed the errors and abuses of the prevailing Mediæval ecclesiasticism; "to which not the superior clergy of that church alone, but the princes as well, from Elizabeth to James Second, clung with such perverse and pernicious tenacity. The great point of divergence and controversy, between the Puritans and their opponents, was *the the right of the civil power*, not to impose articles of belief, but to decree rites and ceremonies, to determine the government of *the church*, to evacuate its discipline, and to dictate its worship. This was what the Crown claimed, what the Court party contended for, and what the Puritans opposed.[10] This, properly speaking, was Puritanism--nothing more, nothing less; it asserted the freedom of the church, from the state and from all despotic Roman ideas--the complete distinction between the civil power and the ecclesiastical, and between their respective spheres of action. That work done, the real posture of Puritanism was defined, and its course closed forever. This explains why MR. HUME,

---

[10] S. P. *Review, Oct.*, 1862 *Art. Puritans.*

the historian, LORD BROUGHAM, and MR. MACAULAY, out of no partiality for the Puritans, unite in the brilliant testimony that, England is indebted to the Puritans for every principle of liberty, in the constitutions of her church and state. Comparatively, the Reformation freed the state from the despotism of the church; Puritanism freed the church from the despotism of the state. The one was the complement of the other; the two were inseparable terms of the same great logic of history, But is not this principle, the freedom of the church from the state, recognized by all among us as a deep-laid element of Southern life? Does it not inhere in the very essence of that life? In denouncing Puritanism, then, we are condemning ourselves, unless we are prepared to renounce that blood-bought *principle*. And surely there is not one who will not declare out of the heart of this civilization--by that principle which affirms that the church shall be free from the state, that the civil power shall never encroach upon the majestic prerogatives of Christ's Crown and Covenant--by that principle I am prepared to stand, and if needs be, I am prepared to die. The Reformers contended for their rights as *thought-men*; The Puritans for their rights as *church-men*; our fathers in the first American Revolution, for their chartered rights as *Englishmen*; but we, merging all these ideas in one, and standing on higher and broader ground--we are contending for our inherent rights as *men simply*; for the rights of self-government that inhere in us organically, and by Covenant as *members of the race*. What relation, then, does Puritanism bear to this Revolution? Are we battling to free the church from the State, or the state from the states? Are we combatting any Mediaeval idea, except that of brutal despotism? What relation then, I repeat, does Puritanism bear to this Revolution, except as it lends a part of the inspiration which the nobler past contributes to the grandeur of the hour?

This view of Puritanism does not imply any approval of the wrong results, to which extremists or the Puritan party, have too often carried their illogical notions. The extremes to which a principle may be carried by professed adherents, are never to be ascribed to the principle itself. Democracy is not republicanism; asceticism is not morality; nor is a rational indulgence in the pleasures of this life, compatible with licentiousness, nor religion with superstition. The principle of Independency is more nearly connected with that of modern philosophical atheism, than with Puritanism. The Independents were but a small segment of the grand Puritan movement. By virtue of other ideas, gotten from the Reformed theology which they held, but afterwards abandoned, they wrought upon the outskirts of that great movement; even as clouds sometimes gather around the mid-day sun. At best, the early settlers of New England, were extremists of the Puritan party. Having approached from another stand-point, though against their knowledge and design, the principle of modern infidelity; they carried an extreme individualism from their doctrine of church-order into theology, into politics, and into social order. After the ridiculous failures in speculative theology of the pigmy imitators of Jonathan Edwards, many of their descendants took refuge from a heartless religion and morality in genteel Deism or sentimental Christianity. Thus, they became more readily receptive of the congenial German Transcendentalism. And when met at last by the alternative of abandoning their doctrine of the church, for one more conservative, as the only means of perfecting and preserving a true theology, or of retaining that doctrine and receiving a deadly philosophy; they accepted the latter and then became, but not till then, the most rotten and malarious element in American civilization. But by the very laws of the moral universe, that principle must needs have run its course; until, like a lawless star or a baleful meteor, it should explode upon some fairest spot of earth, or sink into the blackness of darkness forever. Many of the later and earlier developments of the Plymouth colonists and their descendants, were not the growth of Puritanism. The notorious Code of Blue laws, for example, was not even a natural excresence upon the body; the sickly production of a renegade minister from the Church of England, it had an irregular existence, and then sank into contempt. Did some of the Puritans incur the detestable guilt of persecution? They retaliated upon Cavaliers, the vice which they had suffered at their hands and from whom they learned the art, They persecuted at intervals, through an hundred and fifty years; Cavaliers and Prelates persecuted through hundreds of years, with a ferocity, disarmed at last only by the loss of power. Every sect in Christendom, that has had the power, has likewise persecuted. John Calvin may not be free from the charge of persecution in the case of Servetus; though he certainly is more free than some would insist. Presbyterians of the Established Church of Scotland have conducted legal persecutions against their brethern of the Free Church. Archbishop Laud, of the English Establishment, hunted the Covenanters over the bleak heathers, and through the mountain-gorges of Scotland. The once Established Church of Virginia, persecuted "dissenters" in elder days, side by side with the New England Puritans. But is such violence to be ascribed to the real principles of these parties, or rather to a wrong Mediaeval education, continued through hundreds of years, which taught the doctrine of the divine right of persecution, and from which all Christendom has been slow to recover? It is a savage rule that would defame any class of men, for the crimes of apostate descendants, or for the wrongs of mistaken ancestors. Did the earlier people of New England, remove slavery? They did so chiefly from motives of self interest. Any of these States would do likewise to-day, and the attempt has been made more than once in Southern history. But that is not abolitionism; its principle is that *slavery is sinful in itself, and is therefore a moral, social and political evil*. On the other hand, the ablest defence of the African slave-trade, and, by implication, of the institution of domestic slavery, ever written, emanated from the celebrated divine, JONATHAN EDWARDS; it was reproduced in another less able, by one of his pupils. The recent exertions of such New England men as the REV. DR. LORD, of Dartmouth College, the REV. DR. ADAMS, of Boston, and PROF. S. F. B. MORSE, in the interest of the South, are well known. Least of all has later Now England fanaticism any connection with Puritanism. On the contrary, it has for more than half a century, repudiated every principle of the Puritan faith--all its reverence for the Word of God, for the authority of the Church, for the prerogatives of the King, or of the Constitution. Let it be remembered that the Abolitionism of New England has had an existence of about forty years. Of a purely English origin, it was imported in the doctrines of Wilberforce and Clarkson, and in the lectures of George Thompson. Nor did it take root in the New England mind until, by false philosophies, likewise imported, that mind had been educated away from every principle of its earlier and more conservative, though very defective faith. What I distinctly assert, is that neither the Puritanism of England nor *what there was of Puritanism* in New England, held a single idea in common with Northern fanaticism; that is the growth of European infidelity, favored by the extremes to which the Pilgrims carried the principle of individual liberty. Surely, then, it is to be deeply regretted, that what deserves praise, should have been identified under the name of Puritanism, with that which it abhors, and made the object of indiscriminate denunciation. So far has this noisy spirit gone, as to apply to the late lamented Jackson the epithets "Puritan,"

"Covenanter" "stern Cameronean." As if these terms were synonymous! As if such a cloudlet, from the low grounds of prejudice or ignorance, could do aught else than melt away before undying glory! Let us not be led off by superficial or designing thinkers, from the real causes of our trouble. We are fighting, not Puritanism, but a false philosophy, which would ruin us as it has ruined the great Republic. Nor let us belie the nobleness of Southern character, by upholding such men in flippant or covert calumnies upon illustrious names among the living and the dead.

In this connection let me say a word in passing which is demanded by the simplest justice. Let me not be regarded as a partisan defender of the Puritans, or as speaking in any denominational sense, because I have uttered somewhat in their favor. I speak only in the interest of an enlightened patriotism and common Christianity. Born in the Presbyterian Church; a Southern Presbyterian by the training of my whole life, I have never been identified with the least of Puritan interests through blood or policy. My family blood and the blood of my fathers before me, have been shed for the principles that underlie this Revolution. My own life beats in sympathy with its profoundest elements and yearns for its highest and purest success. As a Presbyterian minister I feel no attraction to such a defence other than that which fidelity to historic truth imposes. It is far from true that the religious economy with which I have the honor to be identified is congenial with New England Puritanism, or was congenital with it, as some would inculcate. Neither was derived from the other; much less are they identical. The Presbyterian system holds but two points in common with the elder Puritanism; namely, the principle of the freedom of the Church from the State, and the doctrine which, as stated by the English Church Puritan Reformers, of the Genevan School of theology, centres in the Seventeenth Article of the creed of the Church of England, and pervades her excellent liturgy. Would it not be a shameful outrage to charge the wrongs of Puritan extremists on that noble church, because Puritanism arose in her bosom, the protest of her evangelical life, embraced many of her noblest intellects, and moved for a time along a common line of history with her; or because among the bitterest enemies of the South is the Cabinet of Great Britain, composed of men, who are English Church-men as well as British diplomatists? Would it not be equally unjust to lay a similar charge upon any American Church, because so many of her clergy and laity have arrayed themselves on the side of New England fanaticism in bitterest hostility to the Confederate States? How much more to charge the errors or even the character of Puritanism upon the Presbyterian Church, because these two systems were at times historically united, when both in their origin, principles, and subsequent career, they have been utterly distinct, and often fiercely antagonistic both in English and American history. Puritanism arose in the latter half of the Sixteenth Century; "the Presbyterian Church was in existence, not in decrepitude, not in decay, but in unimpaired vigor, in uncorrupted integrity, before Henry the Eighth had renounced the supremacy of the Pope; before Calvin had given his immortal institutes to the world, or Luther had translated the Word of God into the German tongue; before the Southern provinces of France had been stained with the blood of the martyred Albigeois; before the morning star of the Reformation had arisen on England; before Charlemagne had restored the Empire of the West."[11] Puritanism arose in England, in the church of England, of which the Puritans were a powerful party; the centre of Presbyterian ideas in that day was Geneva in Switzerland. The Puritans were English, purely English; Presbyterians were chiefly Swiss, French, Scotch and Irish. The fundamental principle of Puritanism was that the Church should be free from all control by the State, and from all Mediæval ideas; the fundamental principle of Presbyterianism has ever been that the written Word of God is the only infallible rule of faith and practice; it fosters proper obedience to appointed constitutional authority in things human and divine. The animus and the specific relations of Puritanism were partly political; Presbyterianism is a system purely religious, evangelical; it, therefore, never has flourished, and never can, in connection with the State. The form of government in

-----

[11] S. P. Review, Oct., 1862, Art. Puritans.

those congregations commonly termed Puritan is a pure democracy, giving unrestrained freedom to all individual tendencies; the form of government in the Presbyterian Church is a representative republicanism, in which all power is conserved in the hands of a few, and individual tendencies are effectually checked by authoritative courts of review and control, combining equal representation from the clergy and the people. We fought the Cromwell Puritans during the civil wars in England; we fought the Independents over the floor of the Westminister Assembly. The famous disruption of the Presbyterian Church in the late United States, into Old and New School, so early as 1837, was the result of an effort on the part of New Englandism, to engraft its radical tendencies on the government, faith and practice of the Presbyterian Church.[12] In this Revolution, the Presbyterian Church in the Confederate States, true to her historic principles, has taken her full share, as one religious element of the South,

---

[12] This statement does not involve the New School Presbyterians of these States, in the charge of fanaticism. Most, if not all, of these withdrew, with the New School party, from the General Assembly of 1837, on the ground that *the exscinding acts were unconstitutional*. On the question of slavery, they separated from the Northern portion of their own body, sometime before the secession of these States from the Federal Union.

of toil and suffering and success. But her record needs no illustration from me. The once living JACKSON, was her type and representative. So in their measure were such as COBB, and SEMMES, and TRACY, and D. H. HILL, and DABNEY CARR HARRISON. Such as INGLIS, of South Carolina, and the lamented YANCEY, of Alabama, NISBET, of Georgia, and TUCKER, of Virginia, have represented in politics, her training. The lamented THORNWELL, of South Carolina, and the living PALMER, of Louisiana, DABNEY, and HOGE, and MOORE, of Virginia, and STILES, of Georgia, have represented her in the pulpit. Her clergy and her people, at home and in the field, have followed these illustrious spirits with utmost devotion to the Southern cause. It is, therefore, a gross historical anachronism, to confound or identify the Presbyterian Church, with Puritanism, real or alleged. The bare intimation of such an idea, is a perversion of historic truth.

My own antipathies, therefore, and they are as stern as the mountain-crags of Scotland, or as the Alps around Geneva--would have induced me, at least, to pass over this popular fallacy with assenting silence. But in considering the subject before us, I found it impossible to avoid noticing the historic posture of Puritanism, because some have labored to force it upon the public mind, in a false relation to this American war. And in presenting such notice, it is equally impossible for any candid student of history, to avoid giving the Puritans their due. Whatever may be our aversion to any phase ofPuritanism, historic fidelity compels the acknowledgement, that the Puritans with all their faults, accomplished great good in their day--they freed the church from the despotism of the State, and I honor them for the work; that they have ceased to be a special influence in American life, for more than sixty years; and they must be denied all claim to a place among the causes that have hurled this appalling crusade upon the existence of the Confederate States. In the name of all that is grand in this Revolution, I enter my protest against the malignant bombast that would degrade it into a renewal of the mythical strife between the Puritan and the Cavalier. It is infinitely removed from that petty feud. Nor does the contest between the Puritans and their real opponents, bear any analogy to this unprecedented struggle, except in the common point of resistance to oppression; though in that point, the analogy is as grand as the issues at stake. Contending, as we are, for the right of self-government, and for purity of faith and practice in politics, in religion, and in social order, we--not the Pantheistic despots of New England--but we of the South, are the Puritans of this controversy, if any Puritans in it there be. Gathering up all the elements of Southern life-- religious, political, and social, against, all the elements at Northern life--religious, political, and social--this Revolution is a grand historic protest against philosophic infidelity and disorganizing wrong. Obeying an imperative historic law, ordained by Providence, it is the inevitable re-action against the extremes of individual power, which are to-day asserted through a lawless

Northern democracy. It aims to save to us all that was true, and to cast out all that was false in the Reformation era. As such, therefore, this Revolution is the van of a great historic movement, whose *design* is to *conserve* all that is precious to living and, for us, to American society--the historic treasures of the past, all the blessedness of the present, and all the hopes of the future.

Considered in reference to American civilization, this Revolution has a more special and, to us, valuable significance. The first epoch of American civilization has just closed.[13] Jamestown and Plymouth Rock, Cavalier and Puritan, Celt, and Teuton, Hollanders and Huguenot, Massachusetts and South Carolina, 1776 and 1812, the purchase of Louisana, the occupancy of the Mississippi Valley, the Mexican War, the Locomotive and the Telegraph--each and all of these historic forces have finished their special works, and gone to make up the distinct and royal personality of an age that has departed. Whatsoever of hope or aim they specially carried has been fulfilled. Whatsoever of true and beautiful, of great and good, distinguished them has been absorbed in the essence of American life; they belong to the massive stratum of the past. "The doctrine of self-sovereignty, first

---

[13] *Atlanta Register, Jan, 5,* 1864. *Philosophy of the Revolution.*

a metaphysical abstraction, then a formal experiment on a scale of magnificence never known in the history of a principle of political science, is now passing through its third stage of development, and today it is stronger than ever before. It is purifying itself by its own action; the action is tremendous, but this only shows the vitality of the sentiment. It is redeeming itself from its own prejudices and passions; the redemption is bloody, but this only shows how tenacious are the issues at stake. Hitherto its battles have been with foreign enemies; against them it has made good its chosen ground, cleaving with its own sword a broad standing-place, and carving out of the materials of half a hemisphere its indestructible fortunes. Now it is self-conflict, the last and perfected form which that disciplinary conflict assumes. As with individuals, so with nations, this law or self-conflict ordained by Providence as a means of discipline, a source of strength, a condition of progress through all the possibilities of growth, presents itself in two distinct forms, the inward and the outward. These are distinct, not separate. Each involves the other; each is a complement to the other. This law of progressive conflict expounds itself in the career of individuals, nations, and religion. It presents its facts over a large surface of human experience, attests its divineness in manifold forms, and challenges our faith by wonders that would be miracles but they belong to a system of uniform action. Under this great law our struggle takes its place. Self-originated, it is self-disciplinary, and hence the very nature of the conflict shuts it up within ourselves, insulates it from foreign sympathy, and resigns the fate of republican liberty to the hands of its immediate friends. The period of American civilization just closed was purely initial and preparatory. It was simply an introductory stage, providentially ordained to effect a certain end and then make way for other and better forms of political and social," of religious and philosophic life. It prophesied a grander and nobler career.

III. This Revolution has a most valuable significance, in that *it aims to conserve the perfection of republican government; and therein to vindicate the organic law, under which civil government was first constituted by God.* That political system, in which each state of a confederacy is balanced against each other state, while each or all of these states combined, are balanced against the central authority to which certain well defined powers are by them delegated, is the perfection of republican government. That system is not democratic, but republican. It involves the doctrine of state sovereignty, "the providential principle of American civilization, and the germ of all the industrial and social grandeur of this hemisphere"--a principle derived from the bosom of European civilization, and which this Revolution will establish upon this continent. It involves *representation*, the political race-feature, of the Anglo-

Saxon race[14]--representation, not of the *individual* directly, but of the state, of classes, through which alone the individual should be felt. Such, contrary to the Northern idea, was the government of the late United States; and but for the poison of foreign and radical ideas, working out through the pestilent heresy of universal suffrage, that government might have proved a success. If the South repeats that heresy, her doom is sealed.

The institution of domestic slavery is an element of inestimable value in our political system. It naturally consigns the whole power of government to the hands of those who are best qualified to use it. The dogma, that all men are entitled to equal rights, is a fatal error. The rights, the liberty which belong to a man, are determined wholly by his character and condition. He is entitled naturally, as a matter of right, to that form of government which is suited to that character and condition. The African slave being unfitted in every respect for self-government, or for

---

[14] We belong to that combination of races which, for want of a better term, we call the Anglo-Saxon race. "In politics, its race-feature is *representation*; in science, induction; in art, utility and then beauty; in society, domesticity; in trade, cosmopolitanism; in religion, protestantism." *Address of the Atlanta Register to the people of the Confederate States*.

a share in the government of others, is, therefore, entitled, as a right, to a complete government by qualified superiors. The system of Bible, domestic slavery is, therefore, the sum of the African's rights, and the sole condition of his welfare. It is not a wrong, nor an oppression to him, but his proper liberty, because it is precisely that form of government which is adapted to his nature and condition, and to which, therefore, he is entitled as a right of nature. It is eminently proper, that society should contain an aristocracy--of virtue, of intellect, of blood and wealth, and worth; and they alone should control the powers of government, because they are most deeply interested in the public weal, and are best qualified to conserve it. The political and social system of these states, this is the finest result of modern political philosophy. It is eminently *conservative*, and eminently suited to the wants of the Southern people. It opposes, on the one hand, the despotism of the individual, which appears in a lawless democracy like that of the United States; it opposes, on the other, the despotism of the mass, which appears in an empire like that of Russia, the only living representative of the extreme of ancient history. With a menial class of contented and governable slaves, whose welfare is ensured by the interest of the owners, it is safe from the danger of popular insurrection, and able to build up a *new, more fruitful and powerful civilization.* Bestowing a complete and adapted liberty on one class, and a complete and adapted slavery on another, it presents the truthful anomaly of a free republican government, resting upon the rightful paradox--liberty and slavery-- proper obedience to qualified superiors. So the universe, with all the systems of truth which it includes, is a system of paradoxes. In religion is the fundamental paradox that God is sovereign, while man is responsible and perfectly free; in philosophy, the paradox that all our knowledge is derived through the senses, and yet man knows nothing, which is not perceived in his conciousness; and the whole system of material nature is governed by the two opposing forces of attraction and repulsion.

Intensely this Revolution is another assertion to the world that--"governments derive their just powers from the consent of the governed"--and that, "whenever any form of government becomes destructive of the ends for which it was instituted, it is the right of the people to alter or abolish it and to institute a new government, laying its foundation on such principles and organizing its powers in such forms, as to them shall seem most likely to affect their safety and happiness." The epithet, *rebels*, so fiercely hurled upon us by the Northmen is sadly amusing when it is remembered, that we are simply contending for the inherent right of self-government, which was so nobly vindicated by their fathers and by ours. The tribunal of history, when it shall come to pronounce upon this Revolution, will convict our enemies of a greater crime than they would fasten upon us. The only expiation they can offer will be a repentance less humiliating than the merciful defeat which awaits them. But higher still, in the sense of a distinguished living speaker;[15]

--"I base the vindication of the South upon a far older record than the Declaration of 1776, and assert her rights under a more authoritative charater than the Federal compact. I affirm that in the organic law under which human governments were constituted by God, not *consolidation* but *separation* is recognized as the regulative and determining principle." From the day when God divided the earth between the Sons of Noah, impressing upon each branch of the race, the character fitting it for its mission; from the day when He dispersed the Babel builders on the plains of Shinar by the radical confusion of human speech; from that day to this the Almighty has ruled the human race and restrained its abounding wickedness by dividing it into parts, and balancing one nation, kingdom, state, against another. I, therefore, recognize in the rupture of the great American Republic a new application of this law, in order to the development of a better life; that Republic had grown too strong for its virtue. And I believe that we have reached one of those great junctures in history, when Jehovah will manifest His own power in the establishment of our independence by the application of this organic law to the conditions of American nationality. "When, therefore, we are aspersed before the tribunal of nations as *rebels* against the Federal government, the Statesman may lay

---

[15] Rev. Dr. Palmer--Same Discourse.

his hand upon the documents drawn up by our fathers, and from them may justify the South; but we may ascend to that fundamental law, by which in the first organization of society God constituted civil government, and say that this law of separation is the 'law of nature and of nature's God,' which entitles us to assume a separate and equal station among the powers of the earth." And yet the American dream of universal empire was not wholly useless. "Impulse and imaginative activity are essential to the first stages of national life; but as we had no feudalism, no crusades, no El Doradoes to furnish this food of lusty growth and exuberant vigor, the enthusiasm of a grand empire, holding half a hemisphere in its grasp, supplied the needed nectar to this modern Jupiter. Its work perfected, its volcanic muscle embodied in iron, its finer ideals sculptured in marable, the great Union passed away."[16] This idea of consolidated power failed even in the congenial Roman life. When wrought upon the church by Hildebrand and his successors, it wrecked her power on the rock-bound shore of the Reformation era. The First Consul sought to enthrone it upon the fickle life of the French; it recoiled before the flames of Moscow; it strewed the fields of Europe with the flower of France; by destiny it was vanquished at Waterloo and then buried with Napoleon at St. Helena. Now we behold the strange anomaly of the United States, a Republic built on the idea of *individual liberty*, asserting every control over the

---

[16] *Address of the Atlanta Register.*

thoughts and the consciences of men, over every interest of society in State and Church, that has been claimed by the worst despotisms of the past. Like all other Babel empires, it must fall before the logic of history. No nation, which identifies itself with an Imperial civilization, or with its congenial element, a despotic churchism, can succeed. Both are at war with the genius of modern history; chiefly for this reason poor Poland has bled and struggled in vain; and sweet Erin lies shorn of her strength and beauty. Let us not be anxious or in haste to form alliances with any of the powers of imperial Europe. Our best dependence is the God of the historic covenant, and the principles which, derived from that covenant, inhere in our civilization and political structure.

IV. This Revolution has an intense significance, in that *it marks the beginning of what certainly seems to be the last period of human history on its or present conditions*. For the reasons suggested in the preceding discussion, it seems proper to describe the present period as the *Period of Conservatism*. The whole tendency of the age is eminently *conservative*. The world everywhere, but especially in these Confederate States, is reacting in one form or other against the extremes of individual authority; and that with an intensity and rapidity which mark no previous era. The United States and England and France, which lead the van of modern civilization, all feel the workings of this intense individualism. Russia, is the only exception, and yet she is fast becoming a part of our actual history. Power has begun a third movement which must complete itself. It will advance, perhaps through many conflicts, perhaps through blood and suffering to its destined end; but harmony will at last crown all human relationships. It would seem also that this is the last period of History; for several reasons which I will briefly mention in closing. If the views of the most sensible and learned students of prophecy during the last three hundred years be accepted as true, we are living in the last day of the World's Prophetic or Sabbatic Week. I do not refer to such writers as the author of Armageddon, nor even to the celebrated Dr. Cummings of London. The latter is a brilliant, cultivated enthusiast; and the theory of the former, though ingenious, is fundamentally untrue. But it is remarkable that the most profound and judicious students of prophecy during the last three hundred years, have referred with singular unanimity to this decade of years between 1860 and 1870, as one that would be marked by decisive changes in Church and State; and would at least set agoing that immediate train of influences which would usher in the millenial era. Some, you are aware, have specially mentioned the years 1866 and 1867 as decisive years; and some have dated from these years the commencement of the millenium itself. This supposition however would seem to be improbable, because the continent of Africa remains to be evangelized before the Gospel-promise can be fulfilled, and this will probably require more than one hundred years for its accomplishment. But still this singular unanimity on the part of most worthy men, impresses us with the conviction that we are indeed living in the last era of human history. Especially was it a favorite idea with some of these men, that the world would last during six periodic days of one thousand years each, and that the seventh thousand years, would be the day of the World's Sabbatic Rest. Now according to *the commonly received chronology* we are living in the last of these Prophetic Days. All the elements of national and historic life which the world can furnish are now employed, so that when the present period shall have done its work, there will remain no new elements or races to take up and complete what we leave undone. What Dr. Arnold beautifully said, twenty-five years ago, concerning modern history in general, may be applied with great force to present history. "I mean that present history appears to be not only *a* step in advance of previous history but *the* last step; it appears to bear marks of the fulness of time, as if there would be no future history beyond it. For the last eighteen hundred years Greece has fed the human intellect; Rome, taught by Greece, and improving upon her teacher, has been the source of law and government and social civilization;" Judea has given to the world a pure Theism and the idea of expiatory sacrifice; and what neither one nor all of these could furnish, "the perfection of moral and spiritual truth, has been given by christianity. The changes which have been wrought, have arisen out of the reception of these elements by new races; races endowed with such force of character that what was old in itself seemed, when exhibited in them, to become something new. But races so gifted are and have been from the beginning of the world few in number; the mass of mankind have no such power; they either receive the impression of foreign elements so completely that their own individual character is absorbed and they take their whole being from without; or being incapable of taking in higher elements, they dwindle away when brought into the presence of a more powerful life, and become at last extinct altogether. Now looking anxiously round the world for any new races which may receive the seed, so to speak, of our present history, into a kindly yet a vigorous soil, and may reproduce it, the same and yet new, for a future period, we know not where such are to be found. Some appear exhausted - others incapable; and yet the surface of the whole globe is known to us. The Roman colonies along the banks of the Danube looked out on the country beyond those rivers, as we look out upon the stars, and actually see with our eyes a world of which we know nothing. The Romans knew that there was a vast portion of the earth which they did not know; how vast it might be was a part of its mysteries. But to us all is explored; imagination can hope for no new Atlantic Island to realize the vision of Plato's Critias; no rising continent peopled by youthful races, the destined restorers of worn-out generations. Everywhere the search has been made and the report has been received; we have the full amount of earth's resorces before us, and they seem inadequate to supply life, for another cycle of human history. I am well aware that to state this as a positive belief would be the extreme of presumption; there may be nations reserved hereafter for great purposes of God's providence, whose fitness for their appointed work will not betray itself until the work and the time for doing it be come. But, without any presumptuous confidenee, if there be any signs, howerver uncertain, that we are living in the last period of the world's history, that no other races remain behind to perform what we have neglected or to restore what we have ruined, then indeed the interest of present history does become intense, and the importance of not wasting the time still left to us many well be called incalculable. When an army's last reserve has been brought into action every single soldier knows that he must do his duty to the utmost; if he can not win the battle now he must lose it. So if our existing nations are the last reserve of the world, its fate may be said to be in their hands--God's work on earth will be *left undone if they do not do it,*"[17]

Such are some of the reflections that have led me to take this view of the meaning of the Southern Revolution. Whether they shall be verified in detail, history alone can determine. But being deeply convinced of at least their general truth, I have ventured to lay them upon your candid consideration. Whatsoever a just criticism may

---

[17] *Dr. Arnold Lectures on Modern History, pgs.* 46-48.

reject, or history may refute, enough will remain to show that the position of the South is sublime. We are leading the great battle for the sum of modern history--for the regulated liberty and civilization of the age It is conservative religion against atheism--constitutional law against fanatical higher law--social stability against destructive radicalism. Upon this conflict, in the highest sense of Napoleon, the eighteen christian centuries are looking down. Our subjugation would be the only inexplicable anomaly of history and its most shameful fact. Nations, one has said, are never murdered; they commit suicide--never destroyed by external power, they sink under their own corruptions and cowardice. If, therefore, the Southern people are what they profess to be; if they are what they have proved themselves to be, through toil, and sacrifice and blood; if they carry any great historic trusts, which are to be held for themselves and their children; if they embody any great principles, which render them worthy of a distinct historic existence; if they are able to be an important element in the civilization of the present age; then is the subjugation of the South an absolute historical impossibility. The independence of these States, is already an established fact; it is ordained by the saving demands of the age, and by the inexorable logic of history. It, therefore, only remains to us to stand in our appointed lot, patient, faithful, till our work is done. Cloudless, happy days are in store for you and your children. Before other battle storms shall beat upon the continent, and perhaps upon the world, let us strive to be where "the wicked cease from troubling, and the weary are at rest."